Holiday Cookies

14 new & delicious cookie recipes (including one for Fido)!

by Hilah Johnson

Other Books by Hilah Johnson

Learn To Cook

The Breakfast Taco Book

Cavelady Cooking!

ISBN: 978-0-9886736-4-9

First Edition: November 2012

Cookie Basics

Here are some tips on making cookies for those who may be new to the activity of cookie making.

Baking Sheets, Greasing and Oven Temperatures

When a recipe tells you to grease or oil a cookie sheet, you can use some spray oil or a dab of vegetable oil or shortening on a wad of waxed paper, smeared all around. I will often use the wrapper from my butter sticks to grease the pans, too. Instead of greasing pans, you can also line them with parchment paper, which is my preference when baking a lot of cookies in one day because after baking, you can lift off the entire sheet of cookies at once and start another batch to bake. Parchment paper can be re-used 3-4 times, as well.

Not all recipes will direct you to grease the pans. High-butter cookies might not require a greased pan to keep from sticking and in fact using a greased pan can cause them to over-spread while baking.

Also make sure to have your oven heated to the correct temperature before putting the cookies in. You could start your oven right when you start mixing the dough, but several of these cookie recipes require the dough to be chilled before baking. Instead, start your oven heating right before you begin shaping the cookies and you won't be wasting a bunch of energy while your dough chills.

Butter

I always use unsalted butter in my baking to prevent overly salty baked goods. I've heard, too, that unsalted butter is fresher because stores can't let it sit around as long on the shelf without the preservative actions of salt.

Most cookie (and cake) recipes will call for "softened butter". Softened butter is room temperature butter and is best gotten to that temperature slowly. If you have the time and forethought, leave your butter out on the counter at room temperature for 30-60 minutes before you begin your recipe. If you don't have the time or forethought, you can soften it quickly by putting a stick of butter, still in its wrapper, in a bowl of warm water for 5-10 minutes; another way is to cut the butter up into cubes and let it sit out at room temperature for 15-20 minutes. When it's soft enough, it will be easy to cut with a butter knife. Beware of letting the butter get so soft it begins to melt (if it's very warm in your kitchen this could happen) because that will affect (though not badly) the texture of your cookies. If you're going to be baking a lot of cookies over a week or so, you might as well just leave a couple pounds of butter out on the counter so it's ready for you when you need it; it won't go off that quickly.

Many recipes begin by "creaming" the soft butter and sugar together, which just means to beat it with a mixer for a minute or so. Creaming the butter this way incorporates air into it, and therefore into the batter to create a light, tender final product with a good rise. To do that: once your butter is softened, place it in a mixing bowl and use a hand mixer (with the standard beaters) or stand mixer (with the paddle attachment) on medium-high speed to beat it until it looks creamy, slightly paler in color, and slightly more voluminous; it will take 1-2 minutes. This can also be done by hand with a wooden spoon and a lot of elbow grease. Now you can add in the sugar if the recipe directs and continue to cream that together. Depending on the butter:sugar ratio in the recipe, you may end up with a light, creamy mixture (high butter) or a mixture that looks like wet sand (high sugar).

Most recipes can be made with margarine or shortening in place of butter, though you should expect some texture and flavor differences than if you use butter. Cream them both the same as you would butter.

Eggs

All recipes were tested using "large" eggs, as that is the standard size in test kitchens. Typically, recipes will direct you to beat in eggs one at a time to ensure thorough mixing.

If a recipe calls for separating egg yolks from whites, the easiest way I've found is to crack the egg and separate into two halves. Allow the white to fall into a bowl, and keep the yolk in one half of the shell. Gently pour the yolk into the other half, allowing the rest of the white to fall into the bowl. Be sure to keep any egg yolk out of the whites if you are planning to beat the egg whites into a stiff meringue. The slightest amount of fat or protein contaminants will inhibit the whites from whipping. For that reason, it's safest to separate each egg individually so that if a yolk does break and fall into the white, at least you won't have to toss all the egg whites and start over.

Flour

In these recipes, "flour" means "all-purpose flour" which is just plain old white flour (as opposed to "whole wheat" and "self-rising" flours). You may use bleached or unbleached flour with no difference in the finished product, though personally I use unbleached flour because, ew, why do I want bleach in my flour? It's plenty white without all that nonsense.

When recipes call for sifted flour: Unless specifically directed otherwise, assume the recipe means you to sift the flour before measuring it. Sifting not only removes lumps, it also aerates the flour and fluffs it up. A cup of unsifted flour weighs more and will contain more actual flour than a cup of sifted flour, though not much more, but it could still affect your recipe. I don't think any of the recipes in this book are that fussy, though.

Sugar

Again, in these recipes "sugar" means "white granulated sugar" — the kind you probably have in your sugar bowl. Generally, turbinado (raw) sugar makes a fine substitute for granulated sugar. Brown sugar comes in both light and dark varieties and while I tested these recipes using light brown sugar, I see no reason you couldn't use dark brown sugar if that's what you have. Your cookies will turn out a little darker and more molasses-y tasting but they'll still be delicious, I'm sure. To properly measure brown sugar, use a dry measuring cup and be sure to pack the sugar in there. Pack it tight then level the top. When you dump it out into your bowl, it should retain the shape of the cup, that's how tight you need to pack it in there to get the right amount.

Baking Soda and Baking Powder

In a nutshell, baking soda is just baking soda (aka sodium bicarbonate or bicarbonate of soda to use an old apothecarial term), while baking powder is a premixed combination of baking soda and an acid. Both of them are "leavening agents" meaning they make things rise and puff up (by producing carbon dioxide bubbles). Baking soda requires the presence of an acid in order to bubble up and do its work, so you will see that recipes calling for baking soda will always have some acidic ingredients (acidic things can be obvious like lemon juice or vinegar, or less obvious like molasses and cocoa). Since baking powder has an acid (usually cream of tartar these days) already mixed in, it will be used for recipes lacking any acidic ingredients. Sometimes you will see recipes that call for both. These are going to be recipes that are only slightly acidic in nature and need a little more "rise" than only baking soda would give when reacting with the small amount of acid.

Cocoa

Cocoa powder in these recipes is always "natural" cocoa powder. You can find (mostly European brands) what's called "Dutch processed" cocoa which is cocoa that's been treated to reduce its acidity. Dutch processed cocoa has a lighter, reddish brown color and a milder flavor than natural cocoa. Because it's also less acidic than natural, be warned that switching one for the other will affect the rise of your baked goods if the recipe relies on the cocoa to react with the baking soda. It's best to use whichever one the recipe calls for; if it doesn't specify, it's safe to assume the recipe means natural cocoa.

Shipping Cookies

Do people still do this? I hope so. It's a wonderful way to share your holiday with someone who can't be there with you but it's also just a nice thing to any time of year. When mailing cookies, choose to include cookies that are sturdy enough to get a little jostled. From this book, those would be Molasses Cookies, Texas Chews, Blueberry White Chocolate Drops, and Reindeer Pellets. In fact, most bar cookies like blondies and brownies also work well. Pack cookies tightly in a plastic or metal canister if possible, putting tissue paper or waxed paper between single layers of cookies. Once your container is packed, put it in a box with some bubble wrap or peanuts around it for cushioning. Mail away!

"Remember When" Cookies

I can only imagine that the person who named these cookies fancied themselves an "old timer" with an appreciation for spice cookies that had been lost on subsequent generations. These cookies are soft and a little chewy and very lightly flavored with anise and coriander; double the spice mixture if you are fond of licorice. Don't be afraid to try these out on people who are not fond of licorice, though. Like I said, it's very subtle. The original cookie recipe called for chopped nuts to be sprinkled atop, but I think sesame seeds look prettier.

You can of course refrigerate the dough longer than an hour, but you will need to let it warm up just a little before rolling. The dough is really pretty easy to work with. The only problem you may encounter is when the dough is very cold it tends to crack rolling. You can easily mash it back together, though, and continue. Scraps can be re-rolled several times with no noticeable difference in the cookies' texture. Store cooled cookies in an airtight container where they will stay fresh and soft for a week or more.

Ingredients

- ¾ cup butter, soft
- ½ cup sugar
- 4 teaspoons honey
- 2 egg yolks (reserve 1 white for later use and maybe use the other to make *Forgotten Cookies!*)
- 2 cups flour (you'll need a little extra for rolling)
- ¼ teaspoon salt
- 2 teaspoons baking soda
- 1 teaspoon ground coriander
- 1 teaspoon anise seed
- 1 egg white
- ½ cup finely chopped nuts or sesame seeds

Instructions

1. Cream butter and sugar.
2. Beat in honey and egg yolks.
3. Add flour, soda, and spices and combine well. Shape into a ball and wrap in plastic.
4. Refrigerate 1 hour.
5. Grease a cookies sheet or line with parchment paper. Set oven to 325ºF.
6. Sprinkle a clean, smooth surface with a tablespoon or so of flour.
7. Roll dough out thin (¼ inch, or just less than 1 cm) and cut shapes. Use a thin spatula to lift the shapes off and place on cookie sheet, ½ inch (1 cm) apart
8. Brush with egg white and sprinkle with nuts or sesame seeds.
9. Bake for 8-10 minutes or until the edges are light brown.
10. Remove and cool completely on racks.

Yield: about 30 - 3" cookies

Moon Cookies

My dad's grandmother made these often so when I was testing recipes for this book, of course he was my test subject for these in particular. He said mine we just like he remembered hers. I couldn't have gotten a better compliment! They are not terribly sweet (which I prefer and so might you if you're feeding these to kids especially) and have a crumbly, shortbread-like texture. Most of the sweetness comes from the powdered sugar dip, an element that also makes them messy to eat. But boy, are they good and pretty!

The dough comes together much like the Mexican Wedding cookies I did in one episode of *Hilah Cooking.* It's stiff. But it can also get a little sticky if your kitchen or your hands are very warm, and it can be hard to form the crescent shapes. If that happens you can always refrigerate the dough for a few minutes. This recipe would be a good one to get kids involved with, too.

Use caution when removing them from the cookie sheets. They are very fragile and have a tendency to break when warm. I recommend letting them cool a few minutes on the sheet before transferring to a rack. And while the original recipe directed that they be rolled in sugar while warm, I had better results coating them after they'd cooled. Or take the middle road and roll 'em in sugar twice!

Ingredients

- » 7 tablespoons granulated sugar
- » 2 cups (1 pound) butter, soft
- » ½ pound almonds, ground (this is almost 2 cups)
- » 3 ½ cups flour
- » 1 cup or more powdered sugar

Instructions

1. Set oven to 350ºF and grease or line a cookie sheet with parchment.
2. Cream butter and granulated sugar together.
3. Add almonds and flour and mix well to form a stiff dough.
4. Pinch off walnut-sized balls of dough — about 1" — and roll between your palms into a short log, about 2" long. Taper the ends and bend into a crescent shape. (An easier way would be to roll them into balls and make "snowball" cookies.)
5. Place cookies on the cookie sheet and bake until lightly browned on bottom.
6. Cool 2-3 minutes on the cookie sheet, then cool on racks.
7. Roll in powdered sugar once cooled.
8. Store in an airtight container in a single layer if possible, or layer waxed paper or parchment between the cookies. They have a tendency to stick to each other if left alone for some time.

Yield: *About 36 cookies*

Thumbprint Cookies

These cookies are not meant to be very sweet on their own, so don't be nervous about the only ½ cup of sugar. The jelly or jam you'll fill them with sweetens them up well. I tried these with strawberry jam, but I think they'd be really nice with lemon curd, pineapple jam, or marmalade, too. I was also thinking if you rolled them in chopped peanuts instead of coconut and filled with grape jelly, you'd have PB&J cookies!

Be sure to keep the egg whites after you separate the eggs; a dip in beaten egg whites before rolling in coconut will help the coconut stick and makes the cookies prettier in the end.

Ingredients

» 1 cup (½ pound) butter, softened

» ½ cup packed brown sugar

» 2 eggs, separate yolks and whites

» 1 teaspoon vanilla

» 2 cups flour

» ½ teaspoon salt

» 1 cup shredded coconut (sweetened or unsweetened)

» ½ cup fruit jam

Instructions

1. Preheat oven to 375° F

2. Cream butter with brown sugar, egg yolks, and vanilla.

3. Add the flour and salt and combine well.

4. Roll into 1" balls, dip in egg whites, and roll in coconut to coat.

5. Bake 5 minutes.

6. Remove from oven and make small indent in top of each cookie. The handle end of a large wooden spoon works well. Though the name implies you should use your thumb, be careful — these will be hot!

7. Cook another 8 minutes.

8. Remove from cookie sheet and let cool.

9. Once cool, fill depressions with a teaspoon or so of any jam you like. If not serving these right away, store unfilled cookies in an airtight container and fill with jam no more than 2 hours before you plan to serve them.

Yield: About 24 cookies

Molasses Cookies

"These smell so good you might not need to eat them!" is the note written on the side of this old card and I completely agree. If you like super crisp and spicy ginger snaps like I do, these are the cookies for you! They will stay good and crisp up to a week if you store them in an airtight container and are sturdy enough to ship so they make a great addition to any care packages you're putting together for holidays.

The original recipe called for melted shortening, which I replaced with oil. If you want to try it with shortening, it was ¾ cup melted and cooled shortening.

Ingredients

- ½ cup vegetable oil
- 1 cup sugar
- ¼ cup molasses
- 1 egg
- 2 cups flour
- 2 teaspoons baking soda
- ½ teaspoon cloves
- ½ teaspoon ginger
- 1 teaspoon cinnamon
- ½ teaspoon salt
- Additional ½ cup sugar for rolling

Instructions

1. Beat oil with sugar, molasses, and egg.
2. Whisk flour with soda and spices and add to wet. Combine well.
3. Chill the dough until ready to cook.
4. When you're ready, set the oven to 375º F.
5. Roll into 1" balls and then roll in granulated sugar. Place on greased or lines cookie sheets, 2" apart.
6. Bake for 10 minutes, then transfer to racks until completely cool. They will be soft at first, but get crisp and dry once cool.

Yield: *About 24 cookies*

Texas Chews

These bar cookies will probably become a year-round cookie for you cookie lovers out there because they're quick, easy, and pretty cheap to make if you leave out the pecans or replace them with peanuts. They are sweet, chewy and gooey so you know the kids will love them. These were the cookies we always made to leave for Santa when I was little, because Santa expressly requested them, of course. For a prettier cookie, you can sprinkle the pecans on top, or dust cooled bars with powdered sugar.

You might get nervous when you peek at them after they've been in the oven for 20 or 25 minutes. The edges might be puffed up high and the center still looks raw, but just give it another 5 minutes. The edges are still puffed up, but the center will be set now. And now we're talkin'. These are also very good served with ice cream, if it's just not enough sugar for ya.

Ingredients

- ½ cup butter or margarine, melted
- 2 cups packed brown sugar
- 2 eggs
- 1 teaspoon vanilla
- 1 ½ cups flour
- 2 teaspoons baking powder
- ½ teaspoon salt
- 1 cup chopped pecans or peanuts

Instructions

1. Preheat oven to 350° F.
2. Combine all ingredients and pat into greased 9 x 13" pan.
3. Bake 25-30 minutes.
4. Cut while slightly warm, but allow to cool completely before trying to remove from the pan.

Yield: 24 bars

Chocolate Chunk Cherry Cookies

This recipe was passed on from my pal Adam. These cookies are amazing and I don't even usually go for that enormous bakery-style cookie. When testing these, I browned the butter as directed here, but Adam said if you don't want to bother, you can just melt it. I also used dried cranberries in place of cherries. Either one is great!

Ingredients

- 12 tablespoons (¾ cup) butter
- 2 cups flour
- ½ teaspoon baking soda
- ½ teaspoon salt
- 1 cup brown sugar
- ½ cup white sugar
- 1 egg
- 1 egg yolk (use the white for another recipe)
- 2 teaspoons vanilla extract, bourbon, or dark rum
- 1 cup bittersweet chocolate chunks or chips
- 1 cup tart dried cherries or cranberries

Instructions

1. Cut the butter into tablespoon pats and place in a heavy-bottomed steel pot or skillet. Put over medium heat and stir until melted. Reduce the heat to medium low and allow butter to cook for about 8 minutes, or until it changes color from golden yellow to sandy brown. Keep an eye on it and reduce the heat to low if the solid particles that settle to the bottom begin to get very dark. Remove from heat and cool for a few minutes.

2. Preheat your oven to 325º F.

3. Whisk flour, baking soda, and salt together in a bowl.

4. In another bowl, mix together the browned butter, white, and brown sugars.

5. Then beat in the egg, egg yolk, and vanilla.

6. Add the dry ingredients into the butter mixture and stir until combined.

7. Fold into the chocolate and cherries. Let the dough rest for at least 10 minutes and up to 30 minutes. This helps the flour absorb the moisture and firm up the dough.

8. Using a ¼ cup measure, portion out your dough onto a greased or lined cookie sheet, 2" apart. These are huge so you will only get about 6 on a standard size sheet.

9. Bake 15 min. The centers will still be soft. Leave them on the sheet until cooled completely.

Yield: *about 16 cookies*

Peppermint Swirls

These pretty peppermint guys make a good use out of the candy canes you buy for decoration, but no one really eats. The log of dough can be kept in the refrigerator for a few days as long as it's tightly wrapped. For a simpler cookie, you could skip the coloring and the layering step and just make regular ice box cookies.

I used my blender to crush the candy canes into powder. The finer you can get them, the easier the cookie will be to slice.

Ingredients

- 10 tablespoons soft butter
- ⅔ cup sugar
- 1 egg
- 2 teaspoons vanilla extract
- 1 ½ cups flour
- 1 ½ teaspoons baking powder
- ¼ teaspoon salt
- 6 tbsp finely crushed candy canes (about 3 full-size candy canes)
- A few drops red food coloring
- *Optional:* red sprinkles

Instructions

1. Cream the butter with the sugar and egg until smooth. Stir in vanilla.
2. Whisk together the flour, baking powder, and salt and add gradually while mixing to the butter mixture.
3. Stir in the candy canes.
4. Remove half the dough from the bowl, put into a small bowl and cover with plastic and refrigerate.
5. Add 3-4 drops food coloring to remaining dough and combine. Once nicely tinted, cover and refrigerate.
6. Refrigerate both doughs for 30-60 min. until firm enough to work with.
7. On a lightly floured piece of waxed paper, roll out the uncolored dough into a rectangle about 10" x 8" x ¼" thick. Set aside. Roll out the colored piece to about the same size.
8. Carefully move the colored dough piece onto the uncolored one and use the waxed paper underneath to help roll it into a log, lengthwise. If you want, you can roll the log in sprinkles at this point. Wrap it up tightly like a piece of hard candy and refrigerate for 4-12 hours.
9. When ready to cook, set your oven to 375°F and prepare two baking sheets with parchment or lightly oil.
10. Slice the log thinly, about ⅛" thick and place on cookie sheets about 1" apart. Bake 8-10 minutes.
11. Cool on racks.

Yield: about 46 cookies

Forgotten Cookies

These are so quick and easy, the hardest part is remembering to take them out of the oven the next day before you start cooking again. Whoops. Did somebody say, "I burned the hay-ell outta these cookies!"?

The original recipe used pecans and vanilla extract, but (while I love them) it's my opinion that pecans get a little over-used around the holidays, especially in Texas. I think the salty pistachios and almond extract work really well, too. Another delicious variation is to use peppermint extract and chocolate chips or white chocolate chips and nix the nuts.

Ingredients

» 2 egg whites
» ½ cup sugar
» ¼ teaspoon almond extract
» 1 cup chopped, shelled pistachios
» 1 cup chocolate chips

Instructions

1. Set oven to 400° F.
2. Beat egg whites until stiff.
3. Beat in salt and sugar and almond extract.
4. Stir in nuts and chocolate chips.
5. Drop by teaspoons onto ungreased cookie sheets, placing about 1" apart.
6. Put in oven and TURN OFF OVEN.
7. Leave in oven overnight. The next day they will be dry and crisp. Store in an airtight container.

Yield: *about 72 cookies*

Blueberry White Chocolate Drops

These have that great "chocolate chip cookie" texture that I love, meaning they're buttery and crisp around the edges and soft and chewy in the center. Try replacing the blueberries with any dried berry for a color and flavor variation. We think the berry flavor in these gets more prominent after a day or two, and that is nice.

Ingredients

» ½ cup (1 stick) softened butter

» ½ cup sugar

» ⅓ cup light brown sugar

» 1 ¼ cups all purpose flour

» ½ teaspoon baking soda

» 1 egg

» 1 teaspoon vanilla extract

» ½ cup white chocolate chips

» ½ cup (3 ounce package) dried blueberries

Instructions

1. Set oven to 350ºF and grease or line cookie sheets with parchment paper

2. Cream butter and sugars together in a large bowl.

3. Beat in egg and vanilla.

4. Whisk flour, baking soda together in a small bowl and add to butter mixture, stirring just until combined.

5. Stir in white chocolate and blueberries.

6. Drop by spoonfuls (about 1.5 teaspoons each) onto baking sheets, 1 ½" apart.

7. Bake 8-10 minutes until light golden brown around the edges.

8. Remove cookies to racks and cool.

Yield: *about 48 cookies*

Apple Oatmeal Cookies

Made with fresh apple and rolled oats, these soft, tender, and chewy cookies are fairly healthy on the health-scale of cookies. Use whole wheat pastry flour and leave out the toffee bits for a cookie that you might could even serve for breakfast! You can totally omit the bread flour from this recipe and just use 1 cup of all purpose flour if you don't keep bread flour on hand. The bread flour makes them a bit chewier, but they are still great without. For a more sophisticated cookie, add in ¼ cup minced candied ginger. Mmm! The apple in these keeps them deliciously moist for up to a week if stored in an airtight container.

Also, this is a great recipe to use any errant jars of Apple Pie Spice you have floating around, getting stale; just use ½ teaspoon pie spice mix in place of the cinnamon and nutmeg.

Ingredients

- ¾ cup all purpose flour
- ¼ cup bread flour
- ¼ teaspoon baking soda
- ½ teaspoon baking powder
- ¼ teaspoon salt
- ¼ teaspoon cinnamon
- ¼ teaspoon nutmeg or ground cloves
- ½ cup (1 stick) butter, softened
- ¾ cup brown sugar
- 1 egg
- 1 teaspoon vanilla
- 1 cup minced fresh apple (about 1 small apple, leave the skin on, cut into ⅛" cubes)
- ½ cup toffee bits
- 1 ¾ cups rolled oats
- *Optional:* ½ cup minced walnuts and/or ¼ cup minced candied ginger

Instructions

1. Set the oven to 350º F and grease or line two baking sheets.
2. Whisk together flour and dry ingredients including spices in a small bowl.
3. Cream the butter and brown sugar together.
4. Add the egg and vanilla and combine.
5. Stir in the flour and mix well.
6. Add in apple, toffee, and oatmeal and combine.
7. To make giganto-cookies: Scoop about ¼ cup of batter onto cookie sheets, 2" apart. Bake for 15-18 minutes or until the edges are brown. The center will still look soft. Allow to cool completely on the pan.
8. To make regular-size cookies: Scoop dough by the teaspoonful onto sheets, 1" apart. Bake for 8-10 minutes or until golden around the edges. Allow to cool completely on baking sheets before removing.

Yield: about 12 giganto-cookies, or 36 regular cookies

Chocolate Coconut Shortbread

These cookies are just as light and crumbly as traditional butter shortbread, with the added flavor of coconut and chocolate. They also happen to be vegan! The traditional ratio for shortbread is 1 part sugar, 2 parts butter, and 3 parts flour. Since butter is only about 80% fat and coconut oil is 100% fat, the ratio had to be adjusted on these. If you want a more chocolatey flavor, you can add an extra tablespoon of cocoa. And if it's a pain in the boot to find cacao nibs and unsweetened coconut where you live, just leave them out and no one will ever know!

This is one recipe where it's definitely unnecessary to grease the pan and even detrimental to the cookies because they can spread too much. Just use parchment or nothing at all. Parchment makes it easier to get off the sheet, though. Way easier.

Ingredients

- ¼ cup unsweetened shredded coconut
- ½ cup brown sugar
- ¾ cup coconut oil
- ½ teaspoon vanilla
- 1 ½ cups flour
- ¼ teaspoon salt
- ¼ teaspoon baking powder
- 1 tablespoon cocoa powder
- ¼ cup cacao nibs

Instructions

1. Set oven to 350ºF. Line two baking sheets with parchment or leave them ungreased.

2. Toast the coconut by putting it in a dry skillet over medium heat for 2-3 minutes, stirring frequently. Remove from heat when you start to see some brown flecks. Leave it in the pan and set aside.

3. In a bowl, cream sugar and coconut oil together then mix in vanilla.

4. Whisk the flour, salt, baking powder, and cocoa together. Add this to the sugar mixture and mix well.

5. Stir in cacao nibs and toasted coconut, if using.

6. Divide the dough into two equal portions and knead each for a few seconds until it comes together into a ball.

7. Put one ball on each cookie sheet and flatten with your hands to a circle about 6" diameter and ½" thick.

8. Bake for 18-20 minutes until edges are lightly browned and the center is set. It won't have changed color much, but will be pretty firm.

9. If you used parchment, you can go ahead and score the discs with a butter knife into 6 triangles. No need to cut all the way through, just about half way. Lift the parchment and cookie together off the sheet and onto a rack to cool. Once cool, you'll be able to snap the circles into portions.

10. If you didn't use parchment, allow the cookie to cool a minute or two then carefully transfer to a wooden cutting board. Score each disc into 6 wedges like above and allow to cool completely.

Yield: 12 cookies

Reindeer Pellets

It's not rocket science, but these peanut butter no-bake cookies, dipped in chocolate and decorated with rainbow sanding sugar look cute, kids love em, and they're easy as you know what.

Ingredients

- ½ cup milk
- ½ cup (1 stick) butter
- 2 cups sugar
- ½ cup cocoa
- ½ cup peanut butter
- 1 teaspoon vanilla extract
- 2 ½ cups rolled oats
- 1 pound dipping chocolate
- Multi colored sanding sugars for decorating

Instructions

1. Combine the milk, butter, sugar, and cocoa in a saucepan and put over medium heat until the butter is melted. Increase heat and bring to boil, stirring constantly.

2. Remove from heat and mix in peanut butter and vanilla.

3. Once fully incorporated, stir in oats.

4. Drop tablespoons of dough onto waxed paper lined sheets. Refrigerate 20 minutes.

5. Melt dipping chocolate according to package directions.

6. You can either gently roll each cookie in chocolate before dusting with colored sugar, or use a spoon to drizzle chocolate over the cookies before decorating.

Yield: about 72 cookies

Apricot Thimble-itas

From Grandma Pauline's collection, these are a little fussy but everyone agrees they're delicious! Soft, fruity, and cake-like, these would be perfect with a cup of hot tea or coffee. One large orange should be enough to supply all the zest and juice you need for the recipe. If you'd rather skip the filling and just use some apricot (or any fruit) jam in its place, that is just fine! No cookie is worth breaking your neck over. You'll need about ⅔ cup of jam.

Also, I literally used a thimble to cut out the holes in the cookie tops (that seems absolutely insane looking back). If you don't have a thimble, use a ½" cookie cutter or cut holes by hand. I think (don't quote me on this, I haven't tried it) you could even just cut an "X" in the cookie tops before baking. They won't look as pretty, but they will taste good.

Ingredients

Apricot filling:

» 6 ounces dried pitted apricots

» 1 ½ cups water

» ½ cup sugar

» 1 tablespoon orange juice

Cookies:

» ½ cup soft butter

» 1 cup brown sugar

» ½ teaspoon salt

» 1 teaspoon orange zest

» 1 egg

» 2 ¼ cups sifted flour (plus more for rolling the dough)

» 1 teaspoon baking powder

» ½ teaspoon baking soda

» 3 tablespoons orange juice

Instructions

For filling:

1. Combine apricots and water in small saucepan and bring to boil. Reduce heat and cook 15 minutes. Drain, reserving the juice.

2. Mash apricots until smooth and measure one cup.

3. Add sugar, juice, and 6 tablespoons reserved cooking water to the one cup of apricots puree and cook over low heat another 15 minutes, stirring frequently. Cool.

For cookies:

1. Beat butter, sugar, salt, zest, and egg together well.

2. Sift dry ingredients together and add half of them to the butter mixture and combine.

3. Beat in the juice.

4. Mix in last of dry ingredients. Form dough into a ball and wrap in plastic.

5. Chill one hour or longer.

6. When ready to cook, set oven to 375º F and grease or line two baking sheets.

7. Sprinkle a clean, smooth surface with a couple tablespoons of flour.

8. Roll out dough ⅛ inch thick on floured board and cut circles, 2 ½".

9. Transfer half the circles to the baking sheets, placing them 1 ½" apart.

10. Place 1 teaspoon apricot filling in the center of those circles.

11. Cut the centers out of the remaining circles using a thimble and place on top of the first circles so the apricot filling shows through.

12. Use a fork or your fingertips to crimp the edges shut.

13. Bake 8-10 minutes. Cool on sheets for 2-3 minutes before removing to racks to cool. Store in a single layer, covered. I think these are best eaten within 3 days.

Yield: *About 24 cookies*

Homemade Dog Treats

My dog loves these! They're very easy and inexpensive and great for dogs who may have allergies to other proteins like chicken or beef. I used whole wheat flour but if your dog has a wheat allergy, you can use ground oatmeal instead. I have a bone shaped cutter that I use; it's about 2 ½" long and I get 8-10 treats out of this much dough. I don't bother re-rolling scraps. Just bake them separately for irregular-but-still-dog-approved treats!

Ingredients

» 2 cans sardines packed in water

» 1 egg

» 1 carrot, grated (about ½ cup)

» ¼ cup minced parsley (great time to use the parsley stems!)

» 1 cup whole wheat flour, divided

Instructions

1. Set oven to 350ºF. Line a baking sheet with parchment or aluminum foil.

2. Drain the sardines and mash them in a bowl with the egg until fairly smooth. It will not look appetizing.

3. Stir in the carrot, parsley, and half a cup of flour. Stir to make a thick dough. It will be sticky. Add in a little more flour if necessary to get it stiff enough to form.

4. For quick treats, just drop the dough by the spoonful (in sizes appropriate for your dog) on the sheet.

5. For shaped treats, pat the dough out on a floured surface to about ½" thickness and cut out shapes with a cookie cutter. Carefully transfer to baking sheet.

6. Bake 10 minutes for small 1" treats and up to 20 minutes for larger 2" shapes.

7. Cool completely then store in refrigerator.

Yield: about 10 large treats or 30 small treats

Thank you for reading this book! I hope you try the recipes out on your family and friends, not just during the holidays, but all year! Nothing says love like homemade cookies.

In addition to writing cook books, I also host an online cooking show called Hilah Cooking. The purpose of the show is to get people excited about cooking with simple, tasty, and unusual recipes. So far we've made over 170 video recipes. You can check them out at hilahcooking.com.

When I'm not writing cook books or making cooking videos, I enjoy long walks, chips and salsa, drinking beer, and bringing home stray dogs.

Hilah

For more great Recipes

Visit HilahCooking.com

New video recipes every Tuesday and Thursday!